D0498172

GREAT FILMMAKERS

JAMES CAMERON

Wil Mara

Published in 2015 by Cavendish Square Publishing, LLC
243 5th Avenue, Suite 136, New York, NY 10016

First Edition

Website: cavendishsq.com

CPSIA Compliance Information: Batch #WS14CSQ

Library of Congress Cataloging-in-Publication Data

Mara, Wil.
James Cameron / by Wil Mara.
p. cm. — (Great filmmakers)
Includes index.
ISBN 978-1-62712-951-0 (hardcover) ISBN 978-1-62712-953-4 (ebook)
1. Cameron, James, 1954- — Juvenile literature. 2. Motion picture producers and directors — Canada — Biography — Juvenile literature. I. Mara, Wil. II. Title.
PN1998.3.C352 M38 2015
791.43—d23

Editorial Director: Dean Miller
Editor: Fletcher Doyle
Copy Editor: Cynthia Roby
Art Director: Jeffrey Talbot
Senior Designer: Amy Greenan
Production Manager: Jennifer Ryder-Talbot
Production Editor: David McNamara
Photo Researcher: J8 Media

The photographs in this book are used by permission and through the courtesy of: Cover and page 1, Jason LaVeris/FilmMagic/Getty Images; John Moore/Getty Images, 5; P199/File: Orangeville ON.jpg/Wikimedia Commons, 7; pagadesign/E+/Getty Images, 8, 12, 24, 28, 54, 58, 64, 66; www.demilked.com/free-paper-textures-backgrounds, 8, 12, 24–25, 28, 54, 58–59, 64, 66;Dmitri Kessel/Time & Life Pictures/Getty Images, 11; Michael Buckner/Getty Images, 16; © Moviestore collection Ltd/Alamy, 19; Eduardo Parra/Getty Images, 21; Orion Pictures/Rudolph, Joyce/Album/Newscom, 23; Mondadori/Getty Images, 25; Columbia TriStar/Moviepix/Getty Images, 27; © AF archive/Alamy, 29; 20th Century Fox/Album/Newscom, 33; Carolco/Rosenthal, Zade/Album/Newscom, 37; Emory Kristof/National Geographic/Getty Images, 39; © Moviestore collection Ltd/Alamy, 40; Mirek Towski/Time & Life Pictures/Getty Images, 41; Apic/Hulton Archive/Getty Images, 42; Imeh Akpanudosen/Getty Images, 45; Buena Vista/Album/Newscom, 46; Vince Bucci/Getty Images, 51; © 20th Century Fox/Entertainment Pictures/ZUMAPRESS.com, 52; © 20th Century Fox/Entertainment Pictures/ZUMAPRESS.com, 56; © 20th Century Fox/Entertainment Pictures/ZUMAPRESS.com, 59; Kevin Winter/Getty Images, 61; ALFREDO ESTRELLA/AFP/Getty Images, 63; AFP/Getty Images, 64.

Printed in the United States of America

GREAT FILMMAKERS

JAMES CAMERON

1	The Immovable Force	4
2	Making His Mark	20
3	Discovery on Film	38
4	The Making of Futuristic Films	50
5	It's A Wrap	60
	Filmography	68
	Glossary	70
	Bibliography	72
	Source Notes	74
	Further Information	76
	Index	78
	About the Author	80

1 THE IMMOVABLE FORCE

Brewing Brilliance

For someone who would later develop a reputation as a stickler for details and a tireless drive toward perfection, it is remarkable to learn that James Francis Cameron entered the world nearly a month late. He was born August 16, 1954, about four weeks past his due date. Yet early on, his potential for creating and developing technology ahead of his time began to surface.

Among his playmates, Cameron became a master builder. He enlisted his friends in projects that included the building of go-carts, boats, rockets, catapults, and miniature **submersibles**. His futuristic drawings and paintings were exhibited in a local gallery when he was still in his teens. It is no surprise that Cameron would later become known for his innovations in movie technology, ambition to make computer graphics look and feel real, and

James Cameron is
Canadian by birth
and spent much of his
childhood in Niagara
Falls, Ontario.

design of a high-definition 3-D camera system. Through his innovations, Cameron would create and direct *Avatar* and *Titanic*, the only two films to break the $2-billion barrier.

Cameron would also develop strong interests in exploring the deep sea, and thereby spend seven years building his own submersible: DEEPSEA CHALLENGER. This development would lead to a partnership with Woods Hole Oceanographic Institution (WHOI) to stimulate advances in ocean science and technology. It would also build on the historic breakthroughs of the 2012 DEEPSEA CHALLENGER expedition—led by Cameron—which explored deep-ocean trenches.

In 2013, Cameron transferred the DEEPSEA CHALLENGER to Woods Hole, where WHOI scientists and engineers currently work with Cameron and his team to incorporate the submersible's numerous engineering advancements into future research platforms and deep-sea expeditions.

Family Ties

Cameron's father, Philip, an electrical engineer, was raised on a farm near Orangeville, Ontario. He received his primary education in a one-room schoolhouse. In true Cameron tradition, he was known for his unflinching points of view and tough-mindedness. And although small in stature, Philip had a powerful personality.

Not long after entering high school, Philip Cameron met the young woman who would become the love of his life, Shirley Lowe. The two were alike in many ways. Lowe was small in stature, had a strong character, and was unafraid to express her

Philip Cameron, James' father, was raised on a farm near the Ontario town of Orangeville.

views. She later became a nurse, and also served in the women's branch of the Canadian military. There was a creative side to Lowe, as she held a strong appreciation for art, music, and film. For many years she painted as a hobby, and studied a variety of subjects for her own pleasure. Lowe and Philip Cameron married not long after graduating from high school. After James, the couple had four more children—Mike, Valerie, Terri, and John.

A Force to Be Reckoned With

Young James Cameron was precocious, creative, and determined. He enjoyed taking things apart to see how they worked. When he became involved with something, he instantly took on the top position and expected everyone around him to follow his direction. When Cameron set his mind to achieve a goal, it was all but impossible to stop him until he'd reached it.

CLAN CAMERON

Although Cameron was born in the central Canadian province of Ontario, he is of Scottish descent. In fact, he is from one of the oldest-known Scottish clans, Clan Cameron, which has a recorded history in the Lochaber region of western Scotland from the fifteenth century. As a Scottish clan, their history is extensive and often combative. They fought in countless Scottish wars and other conflicts through the centuries, most famously with the Jacobite uprisings throughout the 1700s. These battles took place in both Ireland and Great Britain with the goal of reversing the changes in royalty that resulted in the "Glorious Revolution" of 1688. It is likely that some members of the clan were eventually executed for taking what was perceived as a rebellious position on state or religious matters, whereas others were forced to leave the country as a result of their convictions. Thus, in 1825, Cameron's great-great-great grandfather emigrated to Canada to begin life anew.

Cameron was five years old when his family moved from their apartment in Kapuskasing to Niagara Falls, Ontario. Even at that age he was an indifferent student; some of his teachers thought of him as somewhat of a slacker with minimal interest in his lessons. In reality, Cameron, in terms of intellect, was so far ahead of his classmates that he was bored. He skipped a few grades and still didn't feel challenged. He had a particular love for the sciences, and in his spare time he, like his mother, became an enthusiastic reader. Science fiction stories were a particular favorite. He also developed a fondness for history.

Cameron says he was always curious. "I just wanted to know so much and school wasn't getting me there. I mean school was OK, but I wasn't interested in it. I was interested in finding my knowledge through other pathways."

Despite this lack of interest, Cameron was known as a geek. In high school, he started, and was president of, the school's science club. "It consisted of me, and just one girl from Czechoslovakia who didn't speak English—but it was a science club," he said. "All that fed into this need to say something about what I was reading and seeing, and that turned into drawing and painting. And at a certain point in high school I started writing. It wasn't very good; in fact looking back it was pretty terrible. But I had a driving urge to tell stories."

Cameron had ambitions of following in the footsteps of the authors he admired by writing his own science fiction stories. He thought it the perfect blend of his two great passions: science and creativity. He would soon realize that he "saw" his stories, and his urgency to create them would later translate more into making films than writing words on paper. This was a sign of things to come.

"Part of me is just a kid who wants to have these amazing adventures," he admits.

Early Influences

When Cameron was about seven, he saw the 1961 movie *Mysterious Island*. He describes the movie as having "fantastic creature effects in it—really pretty mind-blowing stuff in its day. And I recall that my response to that was to draw. Whenever I saw something that made a strong impression on me I had to draw it. But I wouldn't just draw the thing itself—I would start to embellish and create my own stories around it."

Another of his favorites was *2001: A Space Odyssey*, to which Cameron said he had a "strange reaction. The whole split-scan sequence induced a sense of **vertigo**. I just felt like I was falling. I must have been very impressionable to the physiological effects of movies, and I actually went outside, sat down on the curb in the middle of the day in Toronto and promptly threw up!"

The Way Forward

Cameron had always been a fan of both television and cinema. But it wasn't until the more expansive and refined sci-fi films of the late sixties came to the theater that inspiration struck. In his early youth, sci-fi films were little more than cheesy "B" movies—films that cost little money to make—with somewhat entertaining storylines and poor special effects. The late sixties' sci-fi films had taken a step forward by introducing more imaginative, meaningfully themed stories and effects. While no match for today's technology, these effects were an improvement.

One film that influenced young James Cameron was *2001: A Space Odyssey*.

Cameron was motivated by these films and began seriously thinking about making his own. Using a borrowed **eight-millimeter (8 mm)** camera, he began shooting rough footage. He experimented with lighting, perspective, and special effects. He had fallen in love with *2001: A Space Odyssey* and watched it repeatedly to figure out how some of the key shots were created. He even found a book on the making of the film, which led to his collecting books on general filmmaking techniques. Cameron discovered that he enjoyed the meticulous process of figuring out the fine details of creating a film. Once he had them in his mind they would remain locked there forever.

In a surprising twist of fate, Cameron's father came home one day in mid-1971 and announced that he had been assigned a new job. The family would be moving to Brea, California, which is

THE AMERICAN DREAM

As a Canadian, Cameron said that while he was growing up the phrase "the American Dream" held a negative meaning. "It was this kind of cultural imperialism. I grew up in a border town, on the other side of the border, in Niagara Falls," he explained.

Since the family moved to the United Sates when Cameron was seventeen, he now feels that he is "in my basic genetic nature—much more American than Canadian. I really believe strongly in a lot of the traditional values of this country in terms of respecting individual's rights ... freedom of speech, a lot of things that are in the basic fabric of this country."

located near Hollywood, the filmmaking capital of the world.

Cameron wasn't at first thrilled with his new environment in Brea, but he eventually found his way. He performed well as a student at Fullerton College, where he studied physics and English. When not at school, he loved to visit the film archive at the University of Southern California. Yet at home, Cameron struggled with his relationship with his father, who had hopes that he would enter the engineering profession. Despite his natural talent for engineering and his interest in physics, Cameron's sights remained set on becoming the next big filmmaker. This ambition was often the subject of arguments between Cameron and his father.

"My mom encouraged me to be creative, and my dad did exactly the opposite," Cameron said. "My dad used to take my science fiction books out of my hands and throw them in the trash, saying that they were garbage, that they were rotting my brain. He'd also take my comic books away. He made it the forbidden fruit, which is probably the best thing he could have done."

Meanwhile, Cameron's mother was a solid supporter of her son's drawing and painting. "So I got good dominant genes from both sides," he said.

Lessons Learned

The days after Cameron left college, he said, were frustrating. "I was driving trucks, I was a school-bus mechanic, a precision tool-and-die machinist. I was frustrated because I did not know what I was here for, why I was put on this earth." Yet taking advantage of the reference library at the University of Southern California, he continued painting, drawing, and writing as well as his independent studies of film production.

When Cameron left college, he painted posters for low-budget movies. "I had a little apartment in Tarzana, California, and would paint on the back of the bathroom door. When I wanted to check that the perspective was right in the painting, I would turn the door and look at it in the bathroom mirror. I would see the painting mirror image, and immediately see the flaws."

Looking back on these experiences, Cameron said, "Every single thing that I learned at that time has paid off for me. How to drive a truck, how to be a machinist, being a high school janitor and scraping the gum off the bottom of the desks—even that was something that I value now, something that I needed to go through."

From Words to the Screen

For Cameron, filmmaking seemed the best way to blend his urge to tell stories with the urges to create images. "As a kid I was constantly drawing comic books, and filmmaking was a way to put stories and pictures together. That made sense. And of course the stories I decide to tell were science fiction stories."

Being from a little town in Canada, Cameron says, there was "absolutely nothing in my landscape at that time said that me, or anyone else, from that little town would ever do anything of any significance. But in the other hand, there was nothing saying that we couldn't."

Not long after he sat through several viewings of George Lucas's groundbreaking space epic *Star Wars*

(1977), Cameron decided to enlist in a go-for-broke campaign into the film industry. He decided to take the first step with a short story he'd written entitled "Xenogenesis." It involved a human woman and an engineered man who board a spaceship to search for a new world to inhabit. At the time, Cameron said, "It didn't occur to us that there was a way to make movies where you started small, where you made independent films and you grew from that. We wanted to go straight to *Star Wars*."

Cameron's hope was to turn "Xenogenesis" into a full-length film. However, raising money to finance the project proved challenging. He did manage to convince a group of local dentists, who were looking for some interesting investment opportunities, to give him $20,000—just enough to complete a short segment of the film. The idea was that the investors would review the segment and, if they liked what they saw, provide Cameron the funding to complete the entire film. During the twelve-minute demo, the main character, Raj, battles with a large robot. Cameron and his friends put their all into the production—building **sets** from scratch, creating special effects using outdated technologies and practices—yet the investors decided not to fund the rest of the venture.

Despite the setback, Cameron remained confident in his work. He took the short demo to Roger Corman, the owner of an independent film-production house, New World Pictures. Corman had founded New World in 1970 following a busy career as a **director** and **producer** of low-budget movies. He was known in the business to shoot complete feature-length films in record time, often a few days, and make them marketable. By the 1970s, Corman had become so proficient at thrift and efficiency that

Early in his filmmaking career, James Cameron received a great deal of support from director/producer Roger Corman (left).

he decided to make it the philosophical foundation of his company. In other words, New World was built from the start to produce films at breakneck speed and with very little money. That also meant Corman could not afford to pay his staff much money. He would, however, be happy to teach young, eager newcomers everything they needed to know about the movie business. New World was the perfect place for Cameron to show up in 1979 with a copy of the "Xenogenesis" short under his arm.

The Apprentice

Corman was impressed by Cameron's talent, drive, and ambition, and hired him to build models for his newly created special-effects department. Corman's main interest at the time was having his special-effects team build model ships for a production to be called *Battle Beyond the Stars*. When Corman held a contest among the staff to see who could design the best "lead" ship in the film, it was the young and relatively inexperienced Cameron who took first prize. This caught Corman's attention, and it wasn't long before Cameron, now brimming with confidence, began telling Corman about the problems he saw with the film's upcoming production. Shortly after, Corman made Cameron the film's art director. Cameron seized the opportunity, and spent many nights at the studio.

While the finished film was far from an **Oscar** winner, Corman was impressed with Cameron's creativity, as well as his ability to complete tasks on time and under budget. Some of the people who worked under Cameron weren't particularly thrilled with his no-nonsense, full-tilt approach, but he couldn't have cared less—he was quickly learning that at this stage in his career that the just-get-it-done attitude was the way to get noticed.

By 1981, Cameron had impressed Corman and several others enough to be given his first shot at the director's chair. The opportunity was to direct the sequel to the 1978 low-budget horror film *Piranha*, which did reasonably well in theaters and went on to develop a cult following of films of the **genre**. Cameron's film would be titled *Piranha II: The Spawning*. Cameron knew that he could not be particularly choosy since this was his first chance to direct, but he was appalled at the ridiculous storyline: a scuba instructor, biochemist, and police chief investigate a series of grisly underwater deaths in the Caribbean, eventually uncovering the culprits as a mutant strain of piranha. Nevertheless, Cameron took on a fairly practical view of the opportunity, which paid $10,000. About the experience he said, "If a directing gig opened up, you just took it. You didn't read the **script**. The simple fact that Roger was going to spend money on it was all you needed to know ... and then you learned how to direct."

There are three kinds of pictures, Cameron says. "High-budget movies, low-budget flicks, and no-waste films. I'm a no-waste filmmaker." It was this dedication to perfection that caused Cameron to become embarrassed by the low-quality production of *Piranha II: The Spawning*, as well as the deterioration of his relationship with the film's producer, Ovidio Assonitis. "I was put into an untenable situation and then fired a couple of weeks into the shoot, and the producer took over directing," Cameron said of the fiasco. He left the **location**, in Italy, before the shooting was completed.

A couple of months after the film shooting finished, Cameron traveled back to Rome to find out what really happened, but was not shown any of the film. On edge about his reputation, Cameron "went in and ran the film for myself. It wasn't that bad. All I wanted to know was one simple fact. Could I or could I not do this job?" Unbeknownst to the producer and the crew, Cameron "made a few changes before I flew back. I don't know if the editor ever noticed that I actually fixed a couple of things, but, I had to know whether what they had said was true." To this day, *Piranha II: The Spawning*—also known as *Piranha II: Flying Killers*—remains known as Cameron's first feature film.

While in Italy, Cameron developed a fever, and had a nightmare about an assassin from the future. This dreamed-of character would prove to be the turning point for Cameron's career.

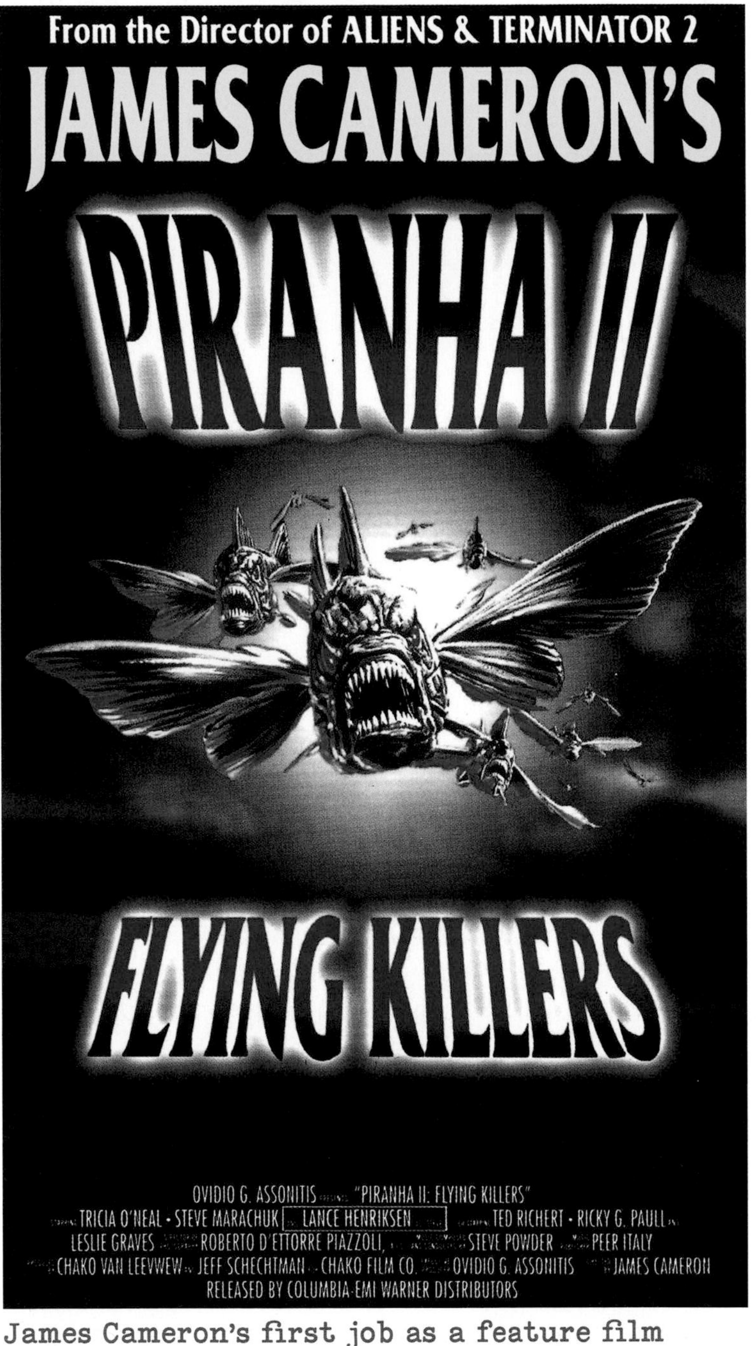

James Cameron's first job as a feature film director was on *Piranha II: Flying Killers*, but he was fired before the movie was finished.

2 MAKING HIS MARK

Dreaming of Success

Many of Cameron's science-fiction stories and images of characters are born in his dreams. Sometimes he writes the events of the dreams down, sometimes he begins to draw or paint.

"I remember very clearly waking up from a dream in college in which I leafed through a book of paintings, waking up and saying, 'Wow, I wish I could paint like that,'" Cameron said. "Then I said, 'wait a minute ... you just painted all those paintings in your head, now paint them for real.' And I quickly painted as many of them as I could remember.'"

One of the paintings was that of a glowing forest with a river of light running through it, with trees that looked like fiber optics. Cut to thirty years later, Cameron said, "and I'm making [*Avatar*], spending millions of dollars to actually create that image—one that came in a dream when I was eighteen years old."

This is one of the robotic hands used in the *Terminator* series, which proved to be James Cameron's first major commercial success.

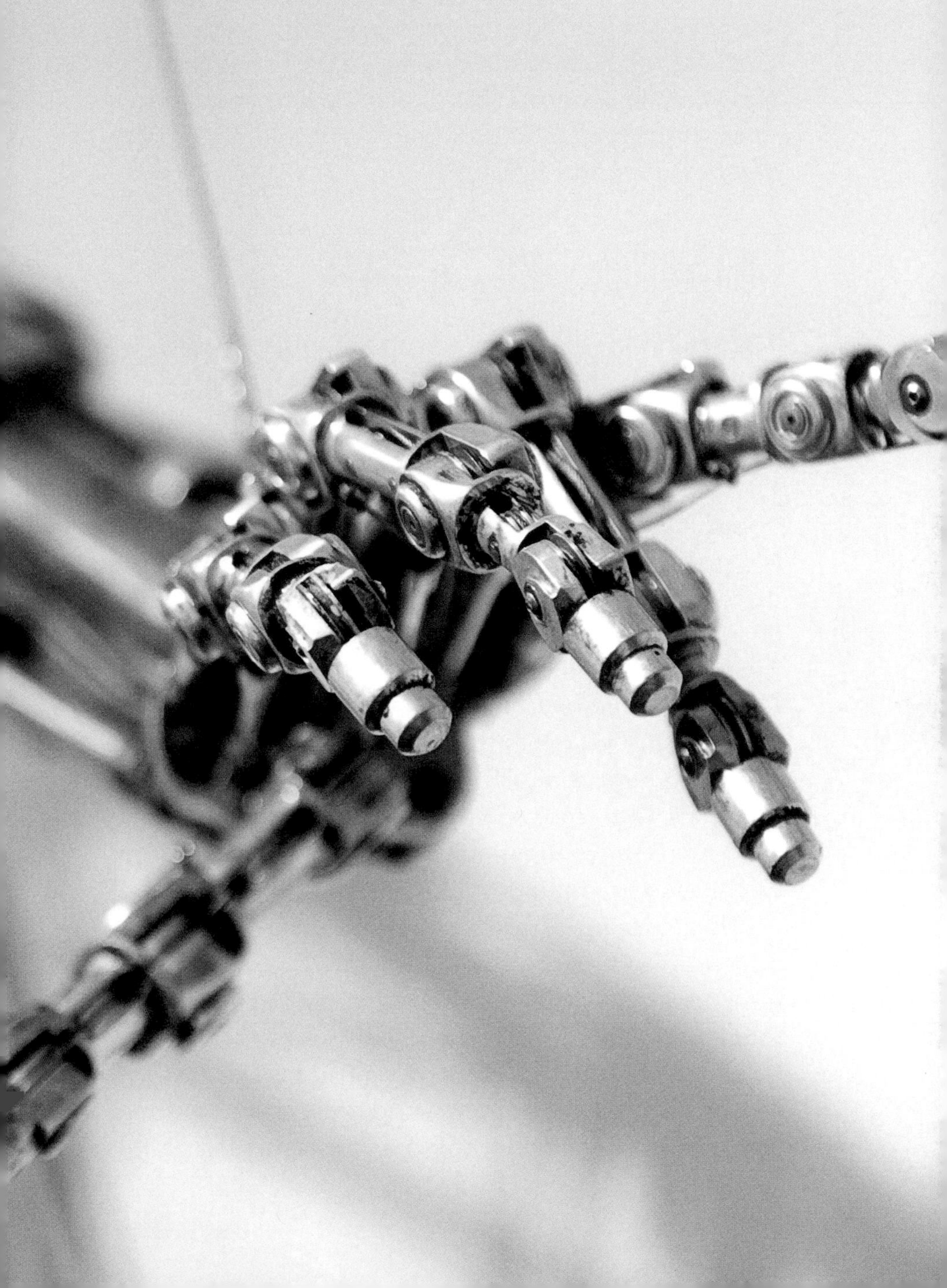

In another such dream, the one he had in Rome, the top half of a humanoid machine was dragging itself out of a fire. Although this was unsettling for Cameron, he began to envision this character as the makings of an intriguing science fiction story. This was the birth of the cyborg—a person whose body contains mechanical or electrical devices—in *The Terminator*. On returning to California, Cameron began writing the script.

From Script to Screen

The setting for the script was in the future, a time during which the human race would be nearly wiped out by cyborgs. When humans begin to fight back, the cyborgs teeter on the brink of extinction. The cyborgs then concoct a plan: send their most efficient killer back in time to murder the mother of the man who leads the fight against the cyborgs. If they kill her, then her son will never be born.

At the time Cameron searched for backers to move the project from script to screen, some of Cameron's friends from his New World days were working for Orion Pictures. With their help, Orion agreed to distribute the film. Cameron also turned to a friend and former coworker from New World, Gale Anne Hurd, to create the screenplay. Hurd would also go on to produce the film.

The script for *The Terminator* was well received. Everybody, Cameron said, wanted to buy it from him, "but nobody wanted me to direct it. They tried to split the team by offering Gale a lot of money."

Hurd was told that she could produce the movie, "but you've got to get rid of him," Cameron said. "But I had actually sold her the rights to the

James Cameron had to meet Arnold Schwarzenegger—and be charmed by him—before casting him in the *Terminator* films.

movie for $1 with the promise that she'd never cut me loose. And she kept that promise. It took two years to get it going. Meanwhile, I was preparing *Terminator* like it was *War and Peace*."

Casting the Cyborg

Originally, Arnold Schwarzenegger was not Cameron's choice for the role of *Terminator*. "I didn't really want him," Cameron said. "Orion had proposed him to play the other guy, because he was the hero." After just one lunch with Schwarzenegger, Cameron changed his mind.

"He was so charming and so into the script and so amusing and entertaining that I totally forgot my agenda," said Cameron. "I had a great time, even though he made me smoke a cigar that made me

A SCI-FI MATCH

Both Cameron and Gale Anne Hurd, who met in 1979, started in the film business working for Roger Corman. The two shared a passion for science fiction, fantasy and action movies, as well as a desire to make them. Cameron said, "I saw in Gale this clarity of purpose, this focus, or, a drive. There was a light behind her eyes that I did not see in any of the other people around me. I watched her work and I saw that she's somebody that makes things happen ... and she was scary smart."

Right after the two met, Cameron said, "I walked out to the curb to get in the car with the guy that I carpooled with ... and I said that she's the one for me. I don't even know what I meant by that at the time, but something told me that there was some type of destiny in that meeting."

Those words soon proved true, as soon after, the pair teamed as director and producer and later married. Although their professional paths would diverge and they would divorce, Cameron "got to watch from afar as she went

Gale Anne Hurd, a successful figure in the movie business in her own right, was James Cameron's second wife.

on to become one of the biggest producers in the business."

Cameron has been married five times: Sharon Williams (1978-1984), Gale Anne Hurd (1985-1989), Kathryn Bigelow (1989-1991), Linda Hamilton (1997-1999), and Suzy Amis (2000-present).

sick for six hours. He even paid for lunch ... I didn't have any money."

Cameron said that he started thinking, "this guy has got the most amazing face. I almost wanted to say, 'Arnold, just stop talking for a second and be real still,' but I was petrified." It was then that Cameron felt Schwarzenegger was perfect for *Terminator*. The deal was closed later that afternoon, and after a two-year hold, the making of the movie began.

The Terminator was released in October of 1984—just over half a year after filming began. It instantly became the number one movie in America. In the first week alone, **box office** earnings were enough to nearly recover all of film's costs. Schwarzenegger's line, "I'll be back," became one of the great movie catchphrases of all time. *The Terminator* would establish Cameron's reputation as someone able to make hit movies.

Tough Men, Tough Women

For his next project, Cameron focused on finishing the script for the second *Rambo* movie. The *Rambo* franchise had been launched in 1982 with the release of *First Blood*, the story of troubled military veteran John Rambo (played by Sylvester Stallone) who has difficulty adjusting to ordinary life back in America. After a series of misadventures and poor decisions, Rambo lands in prison doing hard time.

In the second *Rambo* film, *First Blood Part II*, which Cameron wrote along with Stallone, Rambo is sent to Vietnam in search of American soldiers missing in action. His task is to acquire photos that prove that soldiers are being held captive. Instead,

Cameron worked with screen star Sylvester Stallone in *Rambo: First Blood.*

he helps them escape and is deemed a hero back home. It was released in May 1985.

The success of both *Terminator* and the *Rambo* sequel convinced many in Hollywood that Cameron was a skilled **screenwriter** of blockbusters as well as a capable director.

Cameron quickly began working on his next film, the second of the *Alien* franchise. The first *Alien* film hit theaters in May of 1979 and grew into a science fiction classic. The storyline follows a seven-person crew on a ship returning to Earth after a mining mission to gather minerals. The crew takes a detour, landing on a planet where an alien creature attacks one of its members. He survives the attack but is later killed when a newborn alien, who had been growing inside of him, exits his body. Over time, the rapidly growing creature kills all the remaining crewmembers except Ellen Ripley (played by Sigourney Weaver). In the end, Ripley succeeds in expelling the alien into space and continuing

SIX GUYS IN SUITS

The hundreds of alien creatures shown in the film *Aliens* were actually "six guys in suits," Cameron shared. "There are only six in one shot at one time. It's only editorially that you believe you're seeing more than that because they keep coming at you from different angles."

The point, Cameron said, is that "it requires every ounce of skill, that is my skill as a director, the camera man, the special effects people ... to make those very quick cuts count, to make them as believable as possible." Cameron also said that he tried to make the aliens interesting from a dynamics standpoint. "We did a lot of experimentation in terms of ways of moving them—hanging them on wires, shooting them at different speeds, turning sets upside down and sideways, turning the camera upside down. We used every trick in the book to give them this weird sort of dynamic and un-human type of motion."

Sigourney Weaver reprised the role of Ellen Ripley in James Cameron's *Aliens*.

the voyage to Earth. *Alien* was a massive success, winning countless awards.

Based on *Alien*'s success, Cameron knew he was up against huge odds by agreeing to direct its sequel. This second film, *Aliens*, told the story of Ellen Ripley's return to the planet where she encountered the first alien. The mining company, which has placed a colony there, orders her to go. When Ripley refuses the order, the company assures her that a large team of "space marines" with orders to kill any aliens they encounter will accompany her. But numerous aliens attack this time, and Ripley is once again forced to fight for her life.

Inside the Alien Suit

In filming *Aliens*, Cameron's crew focused more on the movement of the creatures than the design of their costumes. Much time was spent on perfecting their motion because Cameron felt that the quick blurring or insect-like leap was more important in terms of what the audience would enjoy during the film.

Detailed attention on actual costumes, Cameron says, "is the mistake that a lot of make-up and prosthetics people make when they're dealing with this sort of thing. They lavish all their attention on the sculptural detail, the surface texture, etc., of the suit. They fail to realize that people need very few pixels of information to identify a human figure, and most of that identification is through motion. The way we walk, for example, is so engrained in us that you can see it just like that."

Cameron's crew redesigned the suits, made them simpler, less sophisticated, and much more flexible. They then found people to be inside of them. "We hired people who were gymnasts and acrobats—those kinds of things," Cameron explained. "Then we hung them on wires and had them act like lizards. It was a study in motion, in human motion."

Aliens hit theaters in July 1986 and became an instant hit. It received seven Oscar nominations, a rare honor for any science fiction film at the **Academy Awards**. This was no surprise, given that Cameron always wanted to test the limits of possibility.

A Sci-fi Kid

Cameron grew up on "a steady diet" of science fiction. With an hour-long bus ride each way to school, he found himself absorbed in books that "took my mind to other worlds and satisfied, in the narrative form, this insatiable sense of curiosity that I had," he said during his 2010 TED talk.

Growing up in the late sixties, Cameron witnessed American astronauts traveling to the moon, and the deep exploration of oceans. "Jacques Cousteau was coming into our living rooms with his amazing specials that showed us animals and places in a wondrous world that we could never have previously imagined. That seemed to resonate with the whole science fiction part of it."

The Undersea World of Jacques Cousteau (1968–1976), Cameron said, made him excited to think that there is an alien world on Earth. "I might not really go to an alien world on a spaceship someday, but that was a world I could go to right here on Earth.

Underwater Worlds

Watching oceanographer Jacques Cousteau piqued Cameron's interest in the underwater world. "I decided that I was going to become a scuba diver at the age of 15. The only problem was that I lived in a little village in Canada 600 miles from the nearest ocean. But I didn't let that daunt me."

Cameron pestered his father until he found a scuba class in Buffalo, New York, across the border from their Canadian city of Niagara Falls. "I actually got certified in a pool at the YMCA in the dead of winter in Buffalo. And I didn't see the ocean, a real ocean, for another two years till we moved to California."

Since then, Cameron has spent about three thousand hours underwater, five hundred of which were in submersibles, or small vehicles used especially for research that can operate underwater.

He finds the deep ocean environments rich with "amazing life that really is beyond our imagination. I still, to this day, stand in absolute awe of what I see when I make these dives. And my love affair with the ocean is ongoing and just as strong as it ever was."

Creating New Characters

In creating *The Abyss,* Cameron merged his love of underwater diving with filmmaking, and what unfolded was something unexpected. To solve the specific narrative problem in the film—creating the liquid-water creature—Cameron's team embraced computer-generated (CG) animation. This resulted in the first soft-surface character ever in a movie.

Even though the film didn't make any money, Cameron witnessed something he described as "amazing. The audience, the global audience, was mesmerized by this apparent magic. That got me very excited. So I thought that this was something that needs to be embraced into the cinematic art."

With *Terminator 2,* Cameron took this CG effect to another level. Working with Industrial Light and Magic (ILM), he and the team created the film's liquid metal character. "Success hung in the balance on whether that effect would work, and it did," said Cameron. "We had the same result with an audience ... we created a whole new world of creativity for film artists."

Deep-Water Troubles

A significant part of the filming of *The Abyss* took place underwater. Cameron had hoped to shoot the film on location in the Bahamas. When that did not

The shoot for *The Abyss* was among the most stressful James Cameron and his crew ever experienced.

work out, he had two large tanks, which combined held more than 7 million gallons (27,000 cubic meters) of water, constructed specifically for the movie. The location then became an abandoned nuclear plant in South Carolina.

Crews shot an average of fifteen to eighteen hours each day at depths of about 30 feet (9.14 meters) or two atmospheres. To provide the crew with sufficient oxygen to remain underwater for up to five hours, an underwater filling station was constructed.

Maintaining pH levels—a measure of the acidity or basicity of a solution containing or similar to water—was also challenging. Chlorine levels were so high that some crewmembers' hair changed color and fell out. Some experienced burning skin. *Time* magazine reported that during breaks, "the cast and crew emerged from the tanks shaky and unstable, like moonmen readjusting to Earth's gravity. Immediately they climbed into plastic hot tubs, or Jacuzzis, that were set up topside to warm them back up."

The words "The Abyss" had been erased from a blackboard on set and replaced with "The Abuse."

The film's actors wore space-age type helmets that weighed up to 40 pounds (18 kilograms). Each actor required a dive tech assistant to help remove the helmet when they reached the surface. While underwater, dedicated safety divers were assigned to each actor, closely watching his or her every move. Weighted with 40 pounds (18 kg) at his waist and ankles so he could "walk around the bottom of the tank with the camera," Cameron, who could go for about an hour and fifteen minutes on a fill of oxygen, refused a safety diver.

Out of Air

Cameron is known to become deeply absorbed in his work, so he asked his assistant director to warn him when it had been an hour since his last fill. A few weeks into the production, however, a time came when no warning was received.

While directing a scene underwater, Cameron took a breath and sucked in no air. Looking down at his pressure gauge, he saw that it read, "zero." Cameron was 35 feet (11 m) from the surface, and therefore the crew was unable to see his sign for being out of air: a cutthroat motion across the neck and a fist to the chest. Too weighted with equipment to swim to the surface, Cameron was in trouble.

Those working on the set did not have a clear view of him. Luckily, through a sound mixer, a crewmember could hear Cameron removing his helmet as all of its built-in electronics flooded. Cameron then released his buoyancy vest, a type of flotation device, and dropped his helmet to the tank's floor. He then began a "blow and go," a technique used by scuba divers as an emergency procedure when a diver has run out of breathing gas in shallow water and must return to the surface. A safety diver then came to his aid. When the diver attempted to help Cameron, however, Cameron's back-up regulator, or air tank, was broken. Cameron breathed only water into his lungs.

Cameron's scuba diving training in the YMCA's swimming pool kicked in. He broke away from the safety diver, who'd had no idea that Cameron was not getting air, and slowly made his way to the dive platform, where he dragged himself from the tank.

The frightening experience did not hold Cameron back from completing the film. The underwater sci-fi epic opened in theaters in 1989, and went on to win an Oscar for Best Visual Effects.

He's Back

The Terminator franchise would return with the 1991 release of *Terminator 2: Judgment Day*. The target once again is Sarah Connor, mother of the boy who will grow up to lead the resistance against the cyborgs, as well as the boy himself, ten-year-old John. The assassin this time around is not Arnold Schwarzenegger as the Terminator but a more advanced killer made of liquid metal. The Schwarzenegger character is sent to protect the boy.

As Cameron prepared the screenplay, he asked himself, "What's the real goal of this movie? Are we going to blow people away and get them all excited? Is that it? Or is there a way we can get them to really feel something? I thought it would be a real coup if we could get people to cry for a machine. If we could get people to cry for Arnold Schwarzenegger playing a robot, then that would be terrific."

In the first film, the Terminator is not a real character, but a force dubbed the ultimate killing machine, Cameron explained. "He's the embodiment of the ultimate tidal wave, or earthquake, or lightning bolt, or heart attack, the thing you cannot stop. But now, if Arnold was the good guy, then who was the bad guy? How were we going to do this?"

Shifting Animation

The answer was the computer graphics creation of the T-1000—a shape-changing Terminator that could think and mimic the personality of others, which the first Terminator could not do. "But the real horrifying part of the T-1000," Cameron said, "was that you couldn't kill him."

One area in which computer graphics people have been working for a long time is human motion animation. It's been proven to be one of the hardest sciences, "because the eye and the brain inherently know what is right or not right about human beings," Cameron explains. "There's nothing in the world we know more about than the human being. How they move, how they talk, how they smell, how they stand, all of that. We know that at some innate level you can't fool the human eye. So simulating human motion from scratch, mathematically, is very difficult."

Edward Furlong joined Arnold Schwarzenegger for *Terminator 2: Judgment Day.*

In addition to the ability to mimic human motion, T-1000 was a shape-shifter. Yet Cameron felt that there had to be limits. T-1000 could not change its weight or mass because those were physical constants. It could, however, turn into "things," Cameron explained.

Cameron wanted *Terminator 2* to be a significant improvement over the first installment of the movie, as well as to create a character using **computer-generated imagery (CGI)** that audiences would find convincing. He succeeded—the film opened in July 1991, and grossed more than $200 million in the United States.

3 DISCOVERY ON FILM

A Sinking Success

Cameron later focused on creating a movie "about a big ship that sinks." He pitched the idea to studios as being Romeo and Juliet on a ship—an epic romance film. However, Cameron admits that what he secretly wanted to do was "dive to the real wreck of *Titanic*, and that's why I made the movie. And that's the truth."

But Cameron had to convince Paramount Pictures and **20th Century Fox** to back *Titanic*. "I said we were going to dive to the wreck, we're going to film it for real, we'll be using it in the opening of the film ... and I talked them into funding an expedition," he said.

Cameron added, "This goes back to imagination creating a reality ... six months later I find myself in a Russian submersible, two and a half miles down in the North Atlantic, looking at the real *Titanic* through a viewport—not a movie, not HD, [but] for real. Now that blew my mind."

James Cameron confessed that he made *Titanic* because he wanted a reason to explore the wreck of the ship.

Titanic propelled the careers of its two biggest stars—Kate Winslet (left) and Leonardo DiCaprio (center).

Preparation for *Titanic*'s filming, which began shooting mid-1996, was no small undertaking. This included the setting up of underwater cameras and lights, special communications devices, and a replica of the 1912 ocean liner—both inside and out. Thousands of cast members were on set. For the underwater shots, the crew used giant tanks filled with water. Many of the interior sets were rigged for submersion on cue, causing severe damage in the process—just as it happened on the actual *Titanic*. What struck Cameron most about the experience was how much the deep dives were like a space mission.

"It was highly technical and required enormous planning," he said. "You get into this capsule, you go down to this dark, hostile environment where there's no hope of rescue if you can't get back by yourself. I thought wow, I'm living in a science fiction movie—

Titanic earned James Cameron two Oscars.

this is really cool. I really got bitten by the bug of deep-ocean exploration."

Cameron described the *Titanic* experience as one that "Hollywood couldn't give me. I can imagine a creature, and we can create a visual effect for it, but I couldn't imagine what I was seeing out that window ... I was seeing things that I had never seen before. Sometimes [they were] things that no one has seen before—that actually were not described by science at the time that we saw them and imaged them. I was completely smitten."

Titanic won four Golden Globes and received a record-breaking fourteen Oscar nominations, of which the film won eleven—including the Oscar for Best Original Song for "My Heart Will Go On."

After *Titanic*'s success and the discovery of his passion for the deep-sea world, Cameron made the decision to become a full time explorer—for a while.

Battleship Exploration

The Nazi battleship *Bismarck* was launched on May 18, 1941. It was the largest war vessel of its

James Cameron's first project after *Titanic* was a documentary on the German World War II battleship *Bismarck*.

kind ever built. The ship made history during World War II after spending its first eight days cutting a swath of destruction and devastation throughout the North Atlantic. As a result, several Allied ships filled with sailors sank to the bottom of the sea.

But its victories were short-lived. On May 27, 1941, the *Bismarck*, thanks to the combined efforts of the British battleships *Rodney* and *King George*, was defeated and destroyed. When the smoke cleared, the *Bismarck*, carrying 2,106 German sailors, sank. Knowing this piqued Cameron's "explorer curiosity."

Cameron used state-of-the-art technology and filming equipment in the making of the two-hour documentary *Expedition: Bismarck*. In doing so, Cameron and his crew dived some 16,000 feet (4,877 m) into the icy North Atlantic to capture the footage.

He led a team of explorers, historians, and Bismarck survivors to examine the wreck. Historians have long disagreed about what really caused the ship to sink. Evidence uncovered during the exploration suggests that the ship's loss was most likely due to scuttling—a hole cut through the bottom, deck, or side—as originally claimed by her surviving crew members.

Cameron lit up this dark world, providing the first glimpse inside the *Bismarck* in more than sixty years. *Expedition: Bismarck* made its debut on the Discovery Channel on December 8, 2002.

Going Deeper

Cameron and his crew began planning deep-sea expeditions. Using robotic vehicles, they would explore the *Bismarck* and return to the *Titanic* wreck. They created small robots that spooled fiber optics. The idea was to go in and perform an interior survey of the ship, which had never been done.

"Nobody ever looked inside the wreck," said Cameron. "They didn't have the means to do it. So we created that technology to do it."

Cameron found himself on the deck of the *Titanic*, sitting in a submersible. "I was looking out at planks ... where I knew that the band had played. I'm flying a little robotic vehicle through the corridor ... but my mind is in the vehicle."

Cameron said that he felt "like I was inside the shipwreck of *Titanic*. It was the most surreal *déjà vu* experience I've ever had ... I would know before I turned a corner what was going to be there before the lights of the vehicle actually revealed it, because I had walked the set for months when we were making the movie."

About the robotic avatars, Cameron said, "It made me realize the tele-presence experience—

you actually have these robotic avatars, and your consciousness is injected into the vehicle, this other form of existence; it's really quite profound."

Cameron considers the use of the avatars as "a little bit of a glimpse into what might be happening some decades out as we start to have cyborg bodies for exploration in many post-human futures that I can imagine as a science-fiction fan."

Cameron describes the deep-sea creatures studied during his exploration as "aliens living right here on Earth. They live in an environment of chemosynthesis—they don't survive on a sunlight-based system the way we do. You think they can't possibly exist."

A Challenging Journey

After his first plunge into the murky depths at the age of sixteen, Cameron was bitten by the deep-ocean-exploration bug. And that was just the beginning. Later, in 2012, he developed a team of divers who, while exploring the Pacific Ocean's floor, captured hours of video of strange new deep-sea life.

This Mariana Trench dive was done in Cameron's submersible, the DEEPSEA CHALLENGER. The submersible has a vertical design for moving quickly through water. Its hull is made mostly of a foam-like material. Its nearly 7-mile (11-km) descent into the trench took only two hours and thirty-six minutes.

"I was watching the numbers going deeper," Cameron said of the journey. "The sub slows down as you get to the target depth. There is a long moment of getting to think about it. Then you have to get busy. You have less than a thousand feet

To indulge his growing passion for undersea exploration, James Cameron piloted the groundbreaking DEEPSEA CHALLENGER submersible.

from the bottom, you fine-tune the ballast, adjust the camera, turn up the spotlight. As the altimeter counted, I saw the glow of the bottom!"

The six-foot-two Cameron found fitting into the submersible challenging. "I had to keep my knees bent for hours, with only a few inches of arm movement critical to operating the vehicle," he said. Customized cameras inside the high-tech submersible allow documentary viewers to experience the cramped quarters from Cameron's point of view.

This exploration took Cameron 6.8 miles (10 km) to the spot known as the "Challenger Deep" in the trench—an area deeper than Mount Everest is tall. The trip made headlines worldwide. Cameron is the only individual ever to complete the dive in a solo vehicle, and the first person since 1960 to reach the bottom of the world in a manned submersible. Cameron's documentary, *Voyage to the Bottom of the Earth*, chronicles Cameron's historic one-man dive in the trench.

James Cameron teamed with Bill Paxton, one of his stars from *Titanic*, to make the *Ghosts of the Abyss*.

Eyeballing the Wreckage

When Cameron finished *Titanic*, he took a brief hiatus with his brother, Mike Cameron, to relax. The pair embarked on a dive trip. "That's what I do to relax," Cameron said.

With the *Titanic* wreck in mind, he mapped out a model of the vehicle needed to perform a proper and complete archaeological survey of the disaster. It took him from that point almost three years to complete the remotely operated vehicles (ROVs), of which three were created. "They're a very advanced vehicle, in that there are no off-the-shelf components; everything inside it had to be designed from scratch."

Each ROV was equipped with a color and black-and-white camera with the ability to tilt and pan, but the two needed more. "So we created a way of shooting 3-D that is very, very low on eyestrain. You can watch it more or less indefinitely," Cameron explained. *Ghosts of the Abyss*, a 150-minute documentary of this diving adventure, features about 100 hours of handheld work shot by Cameron. It was released by Walt Disney Pictures and Walden Media in April 2003.

Both documentaries were filmed, Cameron said, "for the task itself. It was a challenge. The ocean is the most challenging environment that there is. And this experience has completely changed how I do movies."

Shaking the Ocean Floor

Underwater volcanoes, also called "submarine volcanoes," are commonly found on the ocean floor. Like those on land, some are active and others are not. In shallow water, an eruption may spew steam and debris above the surface of the water. Most, however, lie at such a depth that they can only be detected with proper equipment. This was another wonder that Cameron set out to explore in the 2003 documentary *Volcanoes of the Deep Sea.*

The documentary was intended to introduce audiences to the wonders of the sea, and take them to a place they can't get to themselves. The volcanic world, which has existed for billions of years, could well be the origin of life on this planet, the film's producer Stephen Low says. "It's on the edge of science fiction. There are a lot of things in nature that aren't well understood yet, and a lot of mysteries that haven't been solved."

From these expedition projects, Cameron has learned a lot about leadership, and has been able to incorporate this knowledge into his filmmaking. "I'm not naturally a team leader," he admits. "I don't think I was born a team leader. I think I was born a leader in the sense of having a type of alpha personality, but I don't think I was born with the leadership skills or the leadership impulses. I had to learn it. But that's OK. Everyone has his or her own path."

About filming documentaries, Cameron says, "I enjoy this. It's an alternative to making movies, which are as technically challenging, as emotionally challenging."

A Passion for Space

Cameron has also developed an interest in space science, which led to his involvement with NASA (National Aeronautics and Space Administration) and his becoming a member of the NASA Advisory Council. As a member of the Council, Cameron worked in planning space missions, investigated a camera for a Mars mission, traveled to Russia, and flew to the International Space Station—a habitable artificial satellite in low Earth orbit—with 3-D cameras in tow.

Cameron had always been a "space nut." He cried when, at age fifteen, he watched the launching of Apollo 11. He cried again the first time he saw, in person, a shuttle blast off from Kennedy Space Center, and "felt the vibrations of the sound wave slam into his chest and move right through him."

Combining his passion to explore space and the deep sea, Cameron brought space scientists with him into the deep. Scientists interested in extremophile environments were able to see and take samples of the world below. Extremophiles are organisms that live under extreme environmental conditions such as in a hot spring or ice cap. Through this exploration, Cameron said that he "completely closed the loop between being the science fiction fan as a kid, and doing this stuff for real."

Untouched by Sunlight

In the documentary *Aliens of the Deep*, Cameron teamed with NASA scientists to explore the mid-ocean ridge, an underwater mountain range, formed by plate tectonics. The mid-ocean ridges of the world are connected and form a single global mid-oceanic ridge system that is part of every ocean, making it the longest mountain range in the world. Its total length measures about 37,282 miles (60,000 km). There, many of Earth's more unique forms of life can be found.

Ten hydrothermal vents in both the Atlantic and Pacific oceans are investigated in this documentary. The vents have their own unique ecosystem, which support diverse organisms such as giant tube worms, swarms of blind white crabs, and vast amounts of shrimp. These creatures do not require sunlight like other organisms. Instead they obtain their energy from the vents.

The characters in *Aliens of the Deep* can trump anything that Hollywood can create, Cameron says, "because they're real."

4 THE MAKING OF FUTURISTIC FILMS

Running its Course

Two more installments in the *Terminator* franchise were released during the 2000s—*Terminator 3: Rise of the Machines* (2003) and *Terminator Salvation* (2009). Although both were based on the characters Cameron created, he did not produce or direct either film. Cameron left the *Terminator* franchise in 1991 following *Terminator 2*.

"I have stepped so far away from the *Terminator* universe," Cameron said. "I made a decision a while back to just let it have its life, and from my perspective, it has run its course, and I don't know what more can be said."

Cameron also said that he has no personal desire to return to the franchise, and "certainly [doesn't] want to be a dog in the manger and disallow any of my friends from making money off of it." After the filming of *Terminator 3*, Cameron said that for him, "the story was finished after *T2*."

James Cameron picked up another honor in 2004 at the 30th Annual Saturn Awards.

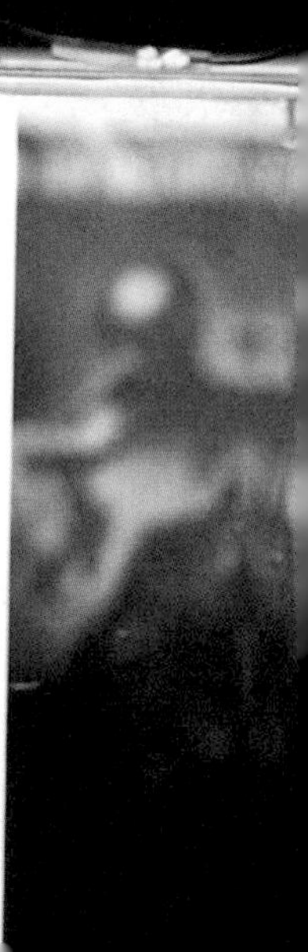

Avatar, with Stephen Lang as Colonel Miles Quaritch, would become one of the biggest hits of James Cameron's career.

Cameron will regain the rights to the *Terminator* franchise in 2019. In the meantime, he worked on what would become his second history-making blockbuster, *Avatar*.

A Blend of History and Nature

Influenced by the history of America being invaded and taken from its indigenous people, Cameron blended the subject in the creation of one of his films: *Avatar*. "I was thinking more about the colonial period," Cameron said about the era in which *Avatar* takes place. "I thought about the French and Spanish coming in and taking over North, Central, and South America; [and] Australia, where they were almost completely genocidal to the Aboriginal people there."

In *Avatar,* the indigenous species of the planet harmonize with nature to fight back against the invading humans. Our track record as human beings, Cameron says, "is pretty bad historically when it comes to a militarily superior society interacting with a society less militarily powerful. They either get wiped out, they get displaced—they wind up either refugees or on reservations. They wind up enslaved. So this is not something we need to feel guilty about, it's just something we need to be aware of."

Cameron viewed the writing of *Avatar* as a way of connecting a thread through history. "I take that thread further back to the sixteenth and seventeenth centuries and to how the Europeans pretty much took over South and Central America and displaced and marginalized the indigenous peoples there."

The human race, Cameron added, has a long history "written in blood going back as far as we can remember, where we have this tendency to just take what we want without asking."

That's not how a just society works, Cameron says, "and we're going to find out the hard way if we don't wise up and start seeking a life that's in balance with the natural cycles of life on Earth."

The lesson in *Avatar,* Cameron says, is one for humankind to stop damaging nature and the environment. "As human beings, we have this kind of sense of entitlement—if we can take it, we will. The major relevance now is that that's our attitude about nature. We just take it. We mine it, we strip it, and we log it. We take from the ocean, we take all the fish, and we don't concern ourselves with sustainability—with giving back that which we've taken. We're going to die out if we don't change our perception."

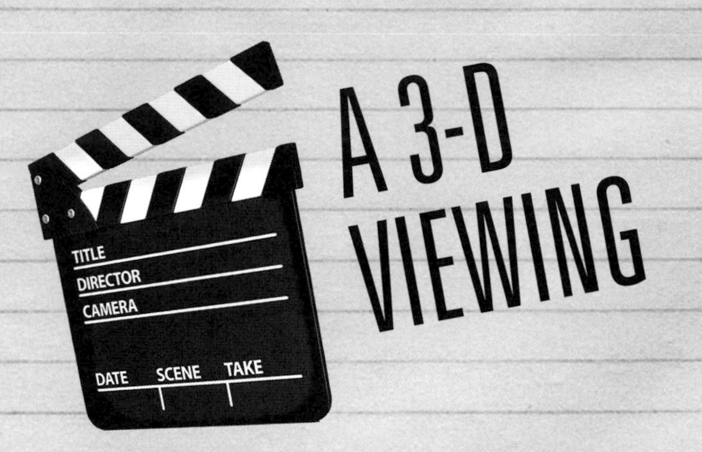

A 3-D VIEWING

Cameron says that when he watches the film *Avatar*, he forgets that it was done in 3-D. "But it's always acting on me, somehow. You're not always aware that the **score** of a film is acting on you. It's there, the music is there, and all this affects your emotions. The 3-D works the same way. It's not that overt, it's not coming at you, or in your face, the whole time, but it's working on your mind the whole time you're watching the movie."

It's absolutely possible that we could see 3-D start to be, instead of in just a handful of films a year, much more the norm, Cameron says. There will come a time when the cinema-going experience "just accepts 3-D where it gets absorbed like color or digital sound. I also don't think it changes the ground rules at all. You still need to have great characters, great stories, beautiful design, beautiful photography—all those things have nothing to do with 3-D."

Creating the World of *Avatar*

Jake Sully (played by Sam Worthington) is *Avatar's* main character. A former marine, he is now a paraplegic who goes into what Cameron describes as "this wondrous world, where you see things in that world that you've never seen before. You fly on a flying creature, become involved in epic battles. It's a love story, an emotional rollercoaster that gets you to the end exhausted. You may even cry once or twice and then wonder 'what the heck did I just see?'"

The techniques used in *Avatar*—the virtual filmmaking, the virtual performance captured on camera, creating its CG template—Cameron says, is "a good way to make a lot of films, whether it's futuristic or in the past. Even a period piece that took place in Ancient Rome or Egypt could use these techniques."

Science fiction works best when you have something that everyone can understand, that everybody can relate to emotionally, and put into a setting that is completely fresh, Cameron said. "And that's what we have here—a main character you can relate to, go [with] on his journey."

Capturing Human Emotion

To depict *Avatar's* alien clan and culture, Cameron thought it would be best to utilize performance capture—a technique of recording patterns of movement digitally, such as the recording of an actor's movements for the purpose of animating a digital character.

"We could have done this with makeup, like it's always been done," Cameron said about creating

James Cameron spent two full years filming *Avatar*.

the characters. However, having actors run around covered in blue paint wearing rubber-like masks, he says, "would have been horrible. I wasn't interested in that. If I was going to do it, I wanted to do it this way—with performance capture." Before Cameron could do that, he had to ensure that his technology could cross what's known in animation and robotics as the **uncanny valley**.

Roboticists believe that when a humanoid robot has an almost, but not perfectly, realistic human appearance, humans will not fully connect with such a robot. This hypothetical relationship between a robot's degree of realism in physical appearance and a human's impression of the robot is called the uncanny valley.

Cameron said that they had to get to "the opposite side where we don't necessarily believe that it's 100 percent photo-real, or that they actually exist, but we have to believe in [the characters] as emotional creatures."

Cameron's crew created a tight-fitting helmet based on a laser scan and life cast of each actor's head. A carbon fiber boom attached to a camera extends in front of the helmet. The camera provides a face shot in a nulled-out close-up. Even though the actor is moving about running, jumping, yelling, and screaming—even jumping off props, jumping over logs, or flat-out running, Cameron says, "We are getting that facial performance absolutely locked off." This allowed for the recording of all facial movements, from the lips to the eyes.

This process, Cameron says, proved to be the "holy grail of how to do CG faces. We got the best animators in the world to take all this data that was coming out of our performance captures, and then we limited their options to things that were value-added, like the ears and the tails. So they took a human performance, with no diminishment whatsoever, and added to it."

When Cameron is asked how much of the performance came through in the characters, he answers, "One-hundred-ten percent. You actually had an increase in the sense of whatever the emotionality of the moment was."

After two years of filming, *Avatar* opened in theaters in December 2009.

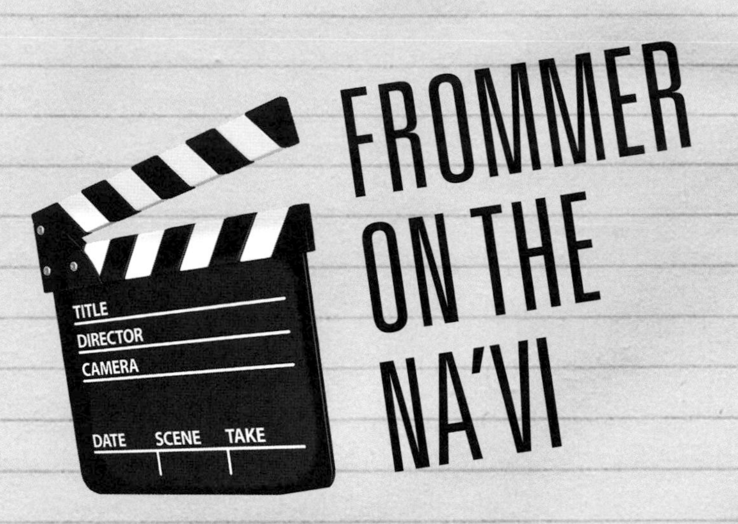

FROMMER ON THE NA'VI

Na'vi is a constructed language spoken by the fictional Na'vi people on Pandora in the film, *Avatar*. Used in the film as well as the subsequent video games, the language was created by Paul Frommer, professor emeritus of Clinical Management Communications at University of Southern California.

Frommer designed the language to fit it to some of Cameron's ideas of how it should sound. It also had to be learnable and pronounceable by the actors.

While working on the set, Cameron asked Frommer, "How do you say 'big blue backside' in Na'vi?"

"I had big, I had blue, but I didn't have a word for posterior," Frommer said. After trying various combinations of sounds, Frommer came up with *eana txim atsawl*.

When a fan asked how to say, "I love you" because he wanted it tattooed on his arm, Frommer said that he "went a bit parental ... I said I'll tell you how to say it, but forty or

Sam Worthington as Jake Sully and Zoe Saldana as Neytiri in *Avatar*.

fifty years from now, do you really think you are going to want to have that tattooed on your body?"

Frommers' favorite Na'vi word is *meoauniaea*, which means "living in harmony with nature."

5 IT'S A WRAP

Return to Pandora

Among Cameron's plans is a return trip to Pandora—three to be exact. He says that his vision for his three sequels is to create a family epic that will introduce viewers to new cultures, and even go underwater on his fictional moon. The filming will take place in New Zealand. The first of the sequels is planned for release in 2016, seven years after the release of *Avatar*. Development of new software for the sequels is under way.

The sequels will include "a lot of new imagery and a lot of new environments and creatures across Pandora," Cameron said. "We're blowing it out all over the place. At first I thought I was going to take it onto other worlds as well, in the same solar system, but it turned out not to be necessary. I mean the Pandora that we have imagined will be a fantasyland that is going to occupy people for decades to come, the way I see it."

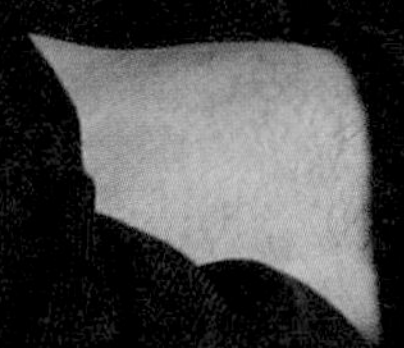

In spite of the massive success he's already achieved, Cameron plans to keep making films.

Water, Cameron points out, is enormously difficult to recreate on a computer. "It's been inaccurately said that the second film takes place underwater—that's not true," he explains. "There are underwater scenes and surface-water scenes having to do with indigenous ocean cultures that are distributed across the three films."

The storyline of the original film was heavily centered on the main character, Jake. Cameron describes it as "his story seen through his eyes." Moving forward, the story will expand. "We spread it around quite a bit more as we go forward. It's really the story of his family, the family that he creates on Pandora—his extended family. So think of it as a family saga like *The Godfather.*"

Avatar's lead characters, Jake and Neytiri, will return in the sequels, as well as many of the humans who caused trouble in the first film.

Dreaming in 3-D

Cameron described making movies as "something great for a techno-geek like me, who loves the hardware, the engineering, and the hard work—the curiosity about how things work." After receiving a positive response from the creators of *Cirque du Soleil* about the possibilities of what 3-D could really be for their audience, Cameron was ready to start filming their performances.

"I'd been talking to *Cirque du Soleil* about doing something in 3-D for a long time," Cameron said. "The *Cirque* guys have shot all their own stuff before, but they never made a movie and they never made it in 3-D."

Cameron described the live shoot as "very, very complicated with a lot of moving pieces, a lot of

James Cameron provided technical help for *Cirque du Soleil*'s 3-D film *World's Away*.

cameras, a lot of technology layered onto the *Cirque* show. It was all unbelievably complex." He embraced his role as executive producer and camera operator "because I love to shoot 3-D. I like to keep my hand in the work, to be on set solving the problems."

The project, which Cameron dubbed "a circus dream," was approached as art and beauty—a type of dreamlike enigma. Ultimately, he said, it's not about that story. It's about the design, the characters, and all the unanswered questions.

"You're kind of in a dream state when you watch a *Cirque du Soleil* show anyway, but now you're being asked to go on a journey between these kinds of circus tents, if you will, in this kind of dreamlike state," Cameron said.

SUSTAINING HOME AND DIET

There is a theme of sustainability that runs through *Avatar*, one that extends into the Camerons' personal lives. Cameron and his wife, Suzy Amis, purchased a farm—their permanent home—located about ninety minutes from the film's Wellington, New Zealand, shooting location, where they will plant 650 walnut trees.

There will also be tree crops, grains, and other produce, Cameron says. "It will be quite a mixed bag. But really, I think of it as an experimental station to look at various sustainable agriculture approaches." The farm, Cameron said, feels like "closing a loop" after he spent summers on his grandfather's farm in southern Ontario.

In 2012, the Camerons adopted a new lifestyle in the kitchen: all-vegan menus. About abstaining from meats, Cameron said, "I felt like I was waking up from a long sleepwalk. I believe we are all sleepwalking off a cliff if we don't do this."

Combined with of the show's color, beauty, and dreamlike presence, the effect of 3-D "just puts you right in the show in a way that I think is even better than sitting in the audience," Cameron said. "You sit in the audience, you see it with one perspective. But you go in with a 3-D camera, and you get in amongst the performers. You get up to those high angles where you really see the jeopardy of those aerial acts; you get above the ground and you feel that sense of vertigo, you appreciate the performances so much more."

There are so many things in *Cirque du Soleil* shows that are never answered for you, Cameron says. "It forces your imagination to kick into gear."

Cirque du Soleil: Worlds Away was released in December 2012.

Coming Full Circle

There's a moment when the fantastic becomes possible, Cameron says. "And that's where the fun is. I think other filmmakers are inherently more brilliant than me, but I know that I can work harder, that I can grind harder than they can."

Whatever tasks Cameron performs or projects he undertakes, he always feels that it is really a quest to learn something. "I don't know where that comes from," he said. "It's somewhere in my Canadian upbringing, somewhere in my family. My dad always instilled in me a strong work ethic when I was a kid. I had a lot of 'stray voltage,' and my parents knew enough to try and put it somewhere."

Cameron credits much of his strength in navigating obstacles and staying focused on surpassing his personal goals to his upbringing.

A MASTER OF SUCCESS

Cameron says that he does not attribute his success to having something to prove. "I don't think of it as having to answer for something. I don't think wow, I got beat up in the ninth grade so I have to show those guys—even though I did get beat up in the ninth grade and it's nice to show those guys. To me that's not what drives it. I think it really is a sense of my craving personal challenge."

When people ask Cameron why he is such a perfectionist, "it's almost like a derogatory connotation. But when you think about the Olympics, what are people striving for—a couple tenths of a second. That makes the difference between you and the guy next to you. That's what everybody's there for, that's what billions of people around the world are tuning in to watch. I think of filmmaking the same way."

Cameron constantly challenges himself artistically, technically, and physically. He thrives on "doing things that are difficult because I know other people are doing them. And maybe that feeds back to some sense of, or maybe lack of confidence." He admits that he does not know how to do anything half way.

As a kid, he says he was "never repressed. And in a funny way I am thankful that I was never helped, I was never given a hand up either because I think there are certain things that you have to build in terms of your will to succeed. And that has to come from self-reliance."

It's critical to have passion in what you're doing, Cameron says. It's critical to have curiosity, work ethic, to set your own personal standards high. "It should never be about money. I'm most proud of the fact that I got to do a lot of things that I really wanted to do, and none of them was making money. Money came because I followed my passion. I went after things that I thought people would be interested in seeing, stories people would be interested in—and they were."

Curiosity is the most powerful thing you own, he says. Imagination is a force that can manifest a reality. As Cameron puts it, "Failure is an option, but fear is not."

FILMOGRAPHY

The following is a selected list of the films James Cameron has directed, written, produced, served as executive producer, worked on, or acted in as of this writing. The films are listed in alphabetical order by year. For a complete listing, please visit the Internet Movie Database website, www.IMDb.com.

Xenogenisis (1978 / director, writer, producer)

Rock n' Roll High School (1979 / production assistant - uncredited)

Battle Beyond the Stars (1980 / special effects)

Escape from New York (1981 / director of photography)

Galaxy of Terror (1981 / second unit director)

Piranha II: The Spawning (1981 / director, writer)

Android (1982 / design consultant)

The Terminator (1984 / director, writer)

Rambo: First Blood Part II (1985 / writer)

Aliens (1986 / director, writer)

The Abyss (1989 / director, writer)

Point Break (1991 / executive producer)

Terminator 2: Judgment Day (1991 / director, writer, producer)

True Lies (1994 / director, writer, producer)

Strange Days (1995 / writer, producer)

Titanic (1997 / director, writer, producer)

The Muse (1999 / cameo)

Expedition: Bismarck (2002 / director, writer, producer)

Solaris (2002 / producer)

Ghosts of the Abyss (2003 / director, writer, producer)

Volcanoes of the Deep Sea (2003 / producer)

Terminator 3: Rise of the Machines (2003 / story inspiration)

The Cutting Edge: The Magic of Movie Editing (2004 / cameo)

Aliens of the Deep (2005 / director, writer, producer)

Explorers: From the Titanic to the Moon (2006 / cameo)

Avatar (2009 / director, writer, producer)

Terminator Salvation (2009 / story inspiration)

Sanctum (2011 / executive producer)

Cirque du Soleil: Worlds Away (2012 / producer)

GLOSSARY

20th Century Fox—One of six major American film studios; the largest in Hollywood.

Academy Award—Any of a series of awards of the Academy of Motion Picture Arts and Sciences in Hollywood given annually since 1928 for achievement in the movie industry in various categories; an Oscar.

box office—A place where tickets are purchased or reserved; gross from ticket sales.

computer-generated imagery (CGI)—Images, both still and moving, created with the aid of computers and then used in a film.

director—The person who oversees the making of a film.

eight millimeter movie camera—A camera that captures motion pictures using eight millimeter film.

genre—A category of artistic composition characterized by similarities in form, style, or subject matter; examples are comedy, science fiction, and documentary films.

location—An actual place where a movie is shot; not a set created in a studio lot.

Oscar—The statuette received when an Academy Award is won.

producer—The person who prepares and then supervises the making of a film before presenting the product to a financing entity or a film distributor.

score—Music written for a movie.

screenwriter—A person who writes the script for a movie.

script—A multipage document outlining the scenes, dialogue, emotions, and other details of a movie.

set—The physical area where a movie is shot.

submersible—A small underwater vehicle that is often used for research.

uncanny valley—The hypothetical relationship between a robot's degree of realism in physical appearance and a human's impression of the robot.

vertigo—A feeling of dizziness associated with looking up or down.

BIBLIOGRAPHY

"10 Questions for James Cameron." Season 2, Episode no. 48, TIME, March 2010. www.youtube.com/watch?v=7yekuJTfddU.

"Aliens Special Edition: Interview with James Cameron." 20th Century Fox, 1986. www.youtube.com/watch?v=9ZzpqZmA2Uc.

Cameron, James, Don Lynch, Ken Marschall, and Parks Stephenson. *Exploring the Deep: The Titanic Expeditions*. San Rafael, CA: Insight Editions, 2013.

Dunham, Brent, ed. *James Cameron: Interviews*. Conversations with Filmmakers Series. Jackson, MS: University Press of Mississippi, 2011.

Grossman, Lev. "James Cameron Almost Died Making The Abyss." *Time*, December 14, 2009.

Heard, Christopher. *Dreaming Aloud: The Life and films of James Cameron*. Toronto, ON: Doubleday Canada, 1998.

"James Cameron: Before Avatar ... a curious boy." TED video, March 2010, 17:08. www.ted.com/talks/james_cameron_before_avatar_a_curious_boy.

"James Cameron Completes Record-Breaking Mariana Trench Dive."

"James Cameron Exclusive Interview." Corporate Valley video, December 9, 2013, 7:21. www.youtube.com/watch?v=F7cLXHYIDeM.

"James Cameron says *Avatar* a message to stop damaging environment." *The Telegraph*, December 11, 2009.

"James Cameron," The Biography Channel website, www.biography.com/people/james-cameron-546570

Keegan, Rebecca. *The Futurist: The Life and Films of James Cameron*. New York: Crown Archetype, 2009.

National Geographic Deep Sea Challenge. "James Cameron." deepseachallenge.com/the-team/james-cameron.

Parisi, Paula. *Titanic and the Making of James Cameron*. New York: Newmarket Press, 2012.

Secret Life of Scientists. "Meet Paul Frommer, Linguist and Inventor of Avatar's Na'vi Language." Science Friday, June 11, 2013.

Turan, Kenneth. "US: James Cameron Interview." Terminator Files, August 1991. www.terminatorfiles.com/media/articles/cameron_005.htm.

SOURCE NOTES

Chapter One

Pg. 9: "James Cameron: Before *Avatar* ... a curious boy," www.ted.com/talks/james_cameron_before_avatar_a_curious_boy.

Pg. 10: "Visionaries: Inside the Creative Mind, James Cameron," www.youtube.com/watch?v=8C74FJNDtLM.

Pg. 12: Realf, Maria, "An audience with James Cameron," www.eyeforfilm.co.uk/feature/2009-12-17-james-cameron-talks-about-avatar-aliens-and-his-titanic-career-feature-story-by-maria-realf.

Pg. 13: "James Cameron Exclusive Interview," www.youtube.com/watch?v=F7cLXHYIDeM.

Pg. 14: Dunham, Brent, ed. *James Cameron: Interviews*. (Jackson, MS: University Press of Mississippi, 2011), p. 143.

Pg. 18: "James Cameron: Interview," www.achievement.org/autodoc/page/cam0int-5.

Pg. 18: "James Cameron: Interview."

Chapter Two

Pg. 20: Turan, Kenneth, "US: James Cameron Interview," www.terminatorfiles.com.

Pg. 22–23: "*Aliens* Special Edition: Interview with James Cameron," www.youtube.com/watch?v=9ZzpqZmA2Uc.

Pg. 34: Grossman, Lev, "James Cameron Almost Died Making *The Abyss*," techland.time.com

Pg. 36–37: Field, Syd, "James Cameron *Terminator 2*: Judgment Day," sydfield.com/interviews/james-cameron-part-2.

Chapter Three

Pg. 38: "James Cameron: Before *Avatar* ... a curious boy."

Pg. 48: Kelly, John, "Director James Cameron Works with NASA on Future Mars Mission," www.space.com

Chapter Four

Pg. 50: Billington, Alex, "Cameron says the *Terminator* Franchise Has 'Run Its Course,'" www.firstshowing.net/2010/cameron-says-the-terminator-franchise-has-run-its-course.

Pg. 53: "James Cameron says *Avatar* a message to stop damaging environment," www.telegraph.co.uk

Pg. 54: Vejvoda, Jim, "James Cameron: *Avatar 4* Possible," www.ign.com.

Pg. 56–57: Seyama, Jun'ichiro, and Ruth S. Nagayama, "The Uncanny Valley: Effect of Realism on the Impression of Artificial Human Faces."

Pg. 58-59: "Meet Paul Frommer, Linguist and Inventor of Avatar's Na'vi Language," www.sciencefriday.com/blogs/06/11/2013/meet-paul-frommer-linguist-and-inventor-of-avatar-s-na-vi-language.html?series=27.

Chapter Five

Pg. 62: Perry, Nick, "James Cameron Wants 'Avatar' To Be Epic Franchise Like 'The Godfather,'" BusinessInsider.com.

FURTHER INFORMATION

Books

Garza, Sarah. *Action! Making Movies*. Huntington Beach, CA: Teacher Created Materials, 2013.

Hamen, Susan. *How to Analyze the Films of James Cameron*. Minneapolis, MN: ABDO, 2011.

MacKay, Jenny. *James Cameron. People in the News*. San Diego, CA: Lucent Books, 2013.

Pletcher, Kenneth, ed. *Explorers in the 20th and 21st Centuries: From Auguste Piccard to James Cameron*. New York, NY: Rosen Education Services, 2013.

Yasuda, Anita. *James Cameron. Remarkable People*. New York, NY: Weigl, 2010.

Websites

James Cameron's Facebook page
facebook.com/JamesCameronDirector

Visit Cameron's Facebook page to view movie clips, production videos, and movie news.

IMDB, James Cameron
imdb.com/name/nm0000116

View photos, videos, and find links to other websites with information about Cameron; learn more about his films.

Box Office Mojo, James Cameron
boxofficemojo.com/people/chart/?id=jamescameron.htm

Explore this online movie publication and box office reporting service website and discover more about Cameron's films, including sales, distribution, and release dates.

INDEX

Page numbers in **boldface** are illustrations

Amis, Suzy, 25, 64
Assonitis, Ovidio, 18

Bismarck, the, 41–43

Cameron, James Francis,
- and the Academy Awards, 30, 31
- and scuba diving, 31–32, 34–35
- as a Canadian, **5**, 8, 12, 31, 65
- as a director, **19**, 24, 27, 28
- as a documentarian, 41–49,
- as a screenwriter, 18, 21, 24, 28, 35
- childhood, 4–13
- early career, 13–32
- filmmaking style, 11, 14–15, 17–18, 20, 22, 27, 28, 29–30, 32–35, 36–37, 40–41, 42, 47, 48, 54–57, 60–63, 65–67

Cameron, Mike, 7, 46
Cameron, Philip, 6–7, 13, 65, 67
Cameron, Shirley Lowe, 6–7, 9, 13, 67
"Challenger Deep," 45
Cirque du Soleil, 62–63, 65
Clan Cameron, 8
computer-generated animation (CG), 32, 55, 57
computer-generated imagery, (CGI), 35, 37
Corman, Roger, 15–17, 24

DEEPSEA CHALLENGER, 6, 44, **45**
Discovery Channel, 45

Frommer, Paul, 58–59

Golden Globes, 41

human motion animation, 36–37
Hurd, Gale Anne, 22–23, 24–**25**

Industrial Light and Magic (ILM), 32

Low, Stephen, 47–48
Lucas, George, 14

Mariana Trench, 44, 46
"My Heart Will Go On," 41
Mysterious Island, 10

NASA Advisory Council, 48
National Aeronautics and Space Administration (NASA), 48
New World Pictures, 15

Pandora, 58, 60, 62
Paramount Pictures, 38

remotely operated vehicles, (ROVs), 46
robotic avatars, 43–44
robotic vehicles, 43

Saturn Awards, **51**
Schwarzenegger, Arnold, **21**, **23**, 26, 36, **37**
submersibles, 4, 32, 38, 43, **45**
sustainable lifestyle, 52–53, 64

3-D film, 6, 47, 48, 54, 62–63, 65
Titanic, the, 38, 39, 40, 43, 46
20th Century Fox, 38
2001: A Space Odyssey, 10, 11

Undersea World of Jacques Cousteau, The, 31
uncanny valley, 56
underwater volcanoes, 47

Walden Media, 47
Walt Disney Pictures, 47
Weaver, Sigourney, 27, **29**
Woods Hole Oceanographic Institution (WHOI), 6

ABOUT THE AUTHOR

Wil Mara has authored more than 150 books, many of which are educational titles for young readers. To find out more about Mara and his work, visit www.wilmara.com.